Printed in the United States of America

First Printing, 2019

ISBN 978-1-7355916-1-2

Independently Published with Kindle Direct Publishing

Book Website: CommonSense-IThink.com

THROUGHOUT YOUR LIFE, you will come across a tremendous amount of people who have a tremendous amount of COMMON SENSE. Now, the reason they have a tremendous amount of COMMON SENSE is because they don't use any of it

UP!!!

***** INTRODUCTION *****

EVERYBODY WILL TELL YOU, they know & understand COMMON SENSE. But is that really reality?

IF IT IS SO, then, why are so many people (& you may know a few) not doing so well in this Great Country concerning the business world...or, even in their personal lives???

I think it lies in one word, "DOING" (PRODUCTIVE)!!!

As we would say down South, "the proof is in the pudding."

SO, I am writing this book in order to try to open up many people's minds. OR, at least one.

THERE COMES a time when someone struggles. There came a time I struggled… way more than one time. There comes a time when even you struggled. But it doesn't have to last long when we use our

COMMON SENSE

COMMON SENSE knows it took time for me, or even you, to get into the problem of being either poor or broke...or both. So, it is easy to assume, it will take us time to become wealthy (well-off).

YES OR NO?

I BELIEVE NOW, I am going to try to keep things Simple & Easy...(now, that does not mean it is Easy & Simple).

FIRST, I am going to stop using the Whole words of

COMMON SENSE

LET me just use the initials of C/S...ok?

SECOND, it will be left up to the readers' own opinions, judgements, thoughts and beliefs to what is being presented in this book. I do not have any desires to explain what is on each page. You, the reader, decide. I know, and I am well aware of it, there will be times when someone will not like what is being written or told.

SHOULD this happen to you, here is what I Suggest. Just tear the Page out of my book & keep on

READING.

THIRD, when I am trying to show C/S on any particular page, I am not trying to put everything in any particular order. I will be trying to give examples of:

***Personal Growth
***Discipline
***Commitment
***Involvement
***Preparation
***Business Behavior
***Business Practices
***Business Philosophies
***Personal Development
***Information vs Knowledge

&

ETC. ---(I just love using that word "ETC")

NOW, it does not take an idiot to read this book. It might take an idiot to write this book----but, that's another story to tell in the future.

I REALLY just wanted to do it so others could enjoy it.

So, don't let me down...

Enjoy it!

Sincerely,
ff6666

TB---------Tom Burns

C/S SEEMS TO KNOW:
BUSINESS
BS*
NOBODY
WANTS YOURS
*Bull Stuff (Polite Way)

C/S WARNS YOU...

The greatest conflicts are not between two people but between one person and himself.

Garth Brooks

Leon M Powell

C/S: Sometimes "Benefits" & "No Benefits" are one and the same.

The Real World of
Work "Benefits"

NOW HIRING!

* 40-60 HOURLY WEEKLY
* LOW PAY SCHEDULE
* NO PAID HOLIDAYS
* NO RETIREMENT PLAN
* NO PAID VACATION
* NO HEALTH BENEFITS
* NO PAY RAISES
* NO PROFIT SHARING

Conclusion: Be careful of what you ask for.

BEWARE of CHICKENS

(AKA, YARDBIRDS)

&

THEIR BUSINESS ATTITUDES

*THEY FOLLOW OTHERS
*THEY ALWAYS DO THE SAME-OLD SAME-OLD
*THEY ALWAYS TRY TO SCRATCH OUT A LIVING (PAYDAY TO PAYDAY)
*THEY DONT SEEM TO HAVE A GOOD PURPOSE IN THEIR LIVES
*LOUD NOISES CAN SCARE THE HELL OUT OF THEM

C/S SAYS,
-ON THE FARM, WHEN IT COMES TO
SURVIVAL, CHICKENS ARE THE FIRST TO GO---ITS ABOUT THE
SAME IN THE BUSINESS WORLD

CS says,

Be prepared in life...

Learn to

DIG YOUR WELL

before you get

THIRSTY

C/S Says:

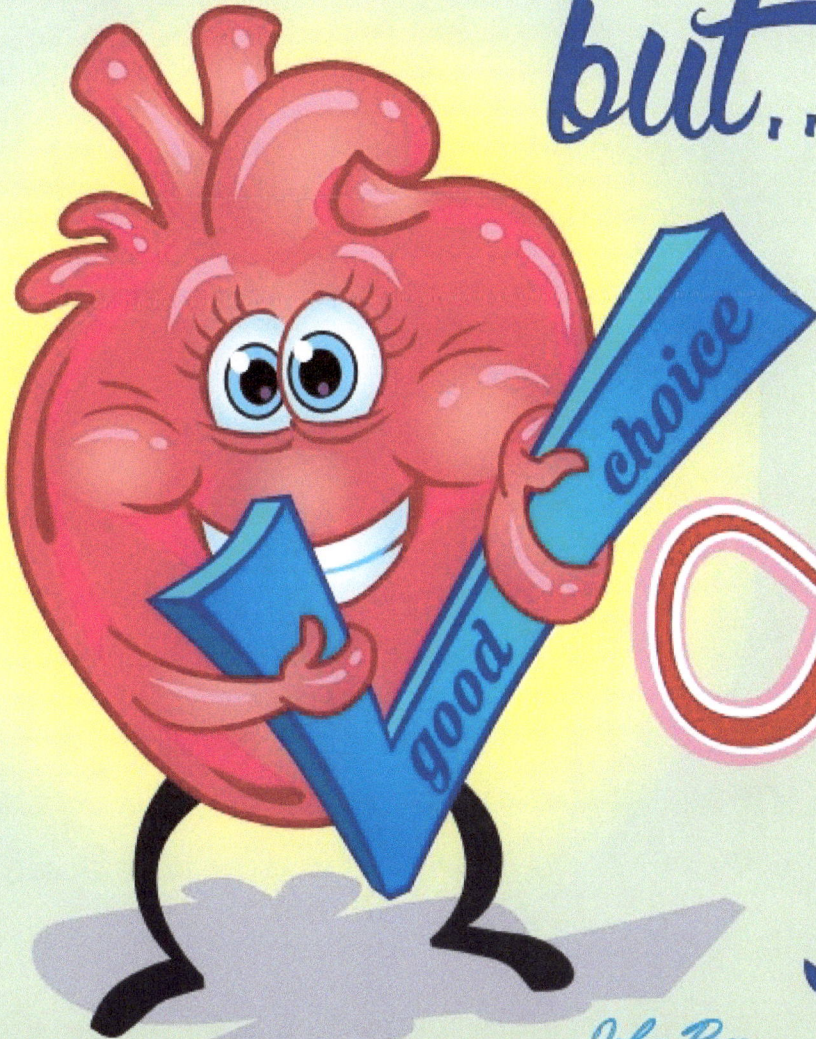

"the Brain Chooses but... the Heart Picks"

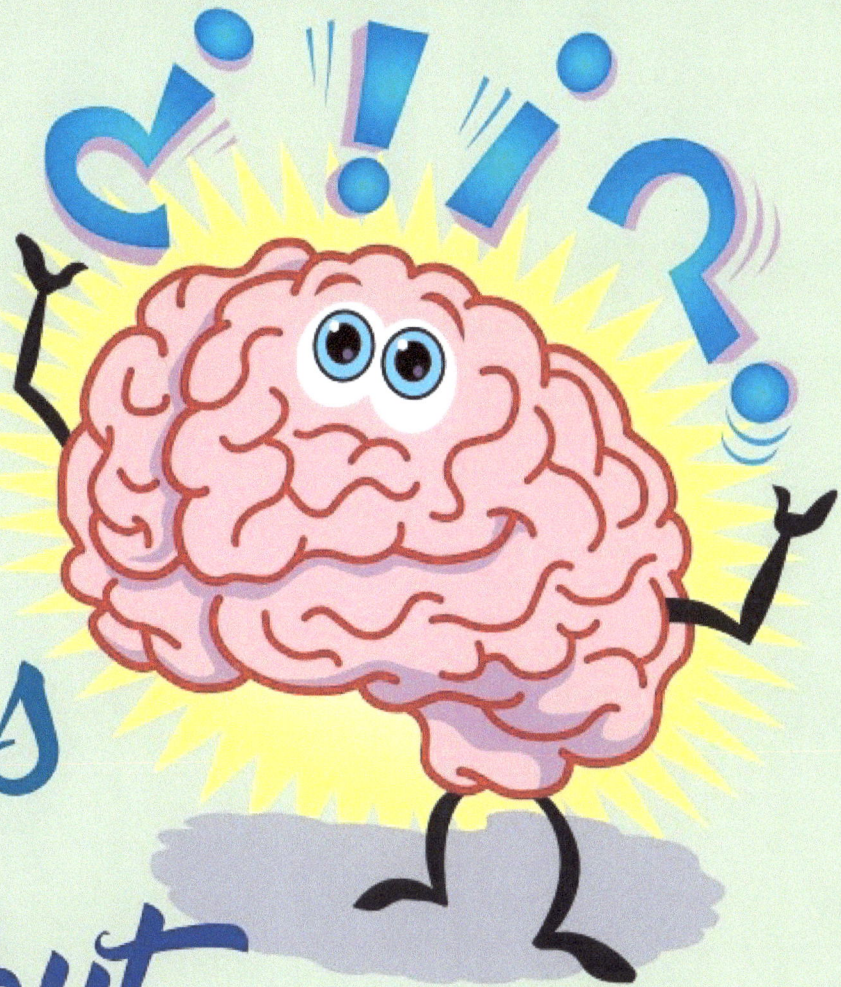

good choice

John Rose

14

LIVING IN THE BUSINESS WORLD WITH...   "4 LETTER WORDS"

15

IN THE BUSINESS WORLD...
NOT 4 LETTER WORDS

BUT SHOULD BE!!

Luck:

Preparation (Growth) +

Attitude + Opportunity +

Action (doing something
about it)

Equals

LUCK

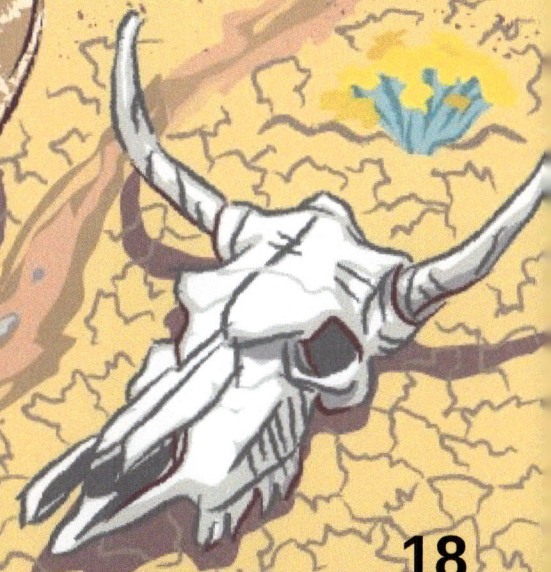

There are those who

are waiting for the

Economy to get Better...

Some people are

Going to have a long wait.

TB

C/S Knows...

Why Fit in when you were Born to Stand Out?

It wasn't God who said that ...
... but He could have.

Dr. Seuss

23

John Roe

DiscomBoBerated

C/S knwos this to be true. You may never

realize it

½
Full

½
Empty

(His)   (Hers)

When you have a crack (flaw) in your
Glass, it doesn't matter what you fill it with,
YOU GOT TROUBLE.

I've never seen a

Person

Die

From trying

But, I've seen

Thousands

Dead (on the inside)

From quitting.

Introduction
Continued,

Well, I reckon it's time to stop talking about

COMMON SENSE

and start talking about

COMMON ENT

and, only one word is needed...

M$NEY

we all want it. Someone get it. Most will not.

...OOPS!!!

almost forgot to tell you, there is no Magic formula to making money. There's no secrets being kept from you on what it takes to make money.

Here is what I have found. And, I know it is "simple & easy". But, unfortunately, it's not "easy & simple". It has been known to those in the business world for hundreds & hundreds & hundreds of years.

The make-up of the "money plan" only consists of 2 words.

AND THEY ARE:

READ

&

LISTEN

Most people, when they graduate from high school or college will never open up another book.

(don't you be one)

I will not waste your valuable time, nor my valuable time trying to explain why people choose to take the negative journey in their lives.

REMEMBER: NO MAGIC

Sincerely,

TB

Tom Burns

No one can get all the information or knowledge in a short period of time. In fact, you will have to use these 2 words, "Read & Listen", for the rest of your life.

So, there is another way to look at what I am saying.

IT'S CALLED

SELF-EDUCATION

Life Is A Number Game

Each Letter Has A Value Equal
To It's Sequence In The Alphabet

A	B	C	D	E	F	G	H	I	J	K	L	M	N	O	P	Q	R	S	T	U	V	W	X	Y	Z
1	2	3	4	5	6	7	8	9	10	11	12	13	14	15	16	17	18	19	20	21	22	23	24	25	26

NEGATIVE

1.)

S	K	I	L	L	S
19	11	9	12	12	19

= 82%

2.)

K	N	O	W	L	E	D	G	E
11	14	15	23	12	5	4	7	5

= 92%

3.)

H	A	R	D		W	O	R	K
8	1	18	4		23	15	18	11

= 98%

BUT,

4.)

A	T	T	I	T	U	D	E
1	20	20	9	20	21	4	5

= 100%

POSITIVE

AND...

5.)

D	O	I	N	G		N	O	T	H	I	N	G
4	15	9	14	7		14	15	20	8	9	14	7

= 128%

VISION

QUESTION: WHAT IS YOUR NUMBER?

God's Gift to us:

Potential

Our gift to God:

Developing it.

C/S says this is not

The End

More Common Sense to come.

ILLUSTRATOR'S CONTRIBUTIONS
(ALL GREAT PEOPLE)

#10) WOODY WOODROME.............

- Page 20........"Pig"
- Page 37........"Zig"

#11) PETER MENICE.............

- Cartoon - Self Portrait

ONE SPECIAL GROUP OF FELLOWS......

***GHANDOLFF THE GRATEFUL

***BOB ANDERSON

***JIM (Sorry. but I honestly don't know his last name)

IDSP BUSINESS ACADEMY MEMBERS
WWW.THEIDSP.NET

This group has used both their talents and time to assist me in creating this book-----all the way from page one to page forty-six. Any entrepreneur who chooses their skills and services will never regret it.

TB

QUOTATION CREDITS

1. Page 9   -   "The Greatest Conflict"   -   Garth Brooks

2. Page 17 -   "Luck" -   Unknown

3. Page 21 -   "Economy -   (me, myself & I) - Tom Burns

4. Page 25 -   "Break Your Neck"   -   Elvis Presley

5. Page 27 -   "Die Trying" -   (me, myself & I again) - Tom Burns

6. Page 38 -   "Potential" -   Alex Sanfilppo

7. Page 39 -   "Have Everything" -   Zig Ziglar

SOMETHING ABOUT ME

I believe I am the type of person who is unshakable in the belief all people are able to do well in life. If, and only if, they use their COMMON SENSE PROPERLY. I feel it is easy to talk about common sense...or, perhaps, "the lack of it".

Throughout my whole business life, this subject seems to come up every day. I think everyone has their own definition of it. So you go ahead and believe whatever you want about it. All I know, it was THE GOOD LORD that gave everyone COMMON SENSE.

This is my first journey in creating a book. I reckon I have been working on it all my life, without knowing it. For the past 40 years, I have been a fan of a thing called Self Education (SE). I have filled many-a empty journal. I have collected several (large) notebooks of ideas, things, samples of what I thought was "good stuff".

Then, about 3 years ago, I was going through them---to see what I would keep and what I would get rid of. Well, a great vision came to me. (Now, I do not remember if I came up with this vision drunk or sober). But one word came to me...PICTURES!!!! Being a country boy, I always like looking at pictures. So, I choose to do a business book with pictures...Illustrations.

Now, I realize all books in the business world that dealt with personal development or business growth contained all words. Well, I thought I would like to do something "u-neek". I would do all pictures. Maybe one day, they will come and "take me away". But until then, I will continue to try fulfilling some of my dreams.

Tom Burns

Book 2

COMMON SENSE & NETWORK MARKETING ARE ONE IN THE SAME

1 of a Kind! Book

1st PRIZE

NETWORK MARKETING & THE GOOD LIFE OR BUST

www.commonsense-

Sample

Tom Burns: The Common Sense

BOOK 3

COMMON SENSE

OR THE LACK OF IT!

"THE COMMON SENSE FELLOW"